USE YOUR VOICE

Written & Illustrated By
KAT KUAN

One Curious Kat - San Francisco Bay Area, CA

Dedicated to
the people
who made me feel
like my voice mattered.

You helped me
find the courage inside myself
to write this book.

Published in the United States of America by One Curious Kat.

First Printing, 2017

ISBN 978-0-9996985-0-1

www.whatkatfoundout.com

Use your voice to say hi.

Use your voice to say your name

GRACE

Use your
voice
to play
with
your
toys.

Use your voice to share how you feel.

SAD

HAPPY